Joke & Riddle Jackpot

Michael J. Pellowski

Illustrations by
Chris Reed

STERLING

New York / London
www.sterlingpublishing.com/kids

To Heidi Goldberg and Lauren Altman
Always Remembered

Library of Congress Cataloging-in-Publication Data
Pellowski, Michael.
  Joke & riddle jackpot / Michael J. Pellowski ; illustrated by Chris Reed.
     p. cm.
  Includes index.
  ISBN 1-4027-1696-6
  1. Riddles, Juvenile. 2. Wit and humor, Juvenile. I. Title: Joke and riddle jackpot. II. Reed, Chris. III. Title.

  PN6371.5.P43 2005
  818'.5402--dc22

                                      2004029879

STERLING and the distinctive Sterling logo are registered trademarks of Sterling Publishing Co., Inc.

Lot #:
10 9 8 7 6 5 4 3 2
04/11
Published by Sterling Publishing Co., Inc.
387 Park Avenue South, New York, NY 10016

Distributed in Canada by Sterling Publishing
c/o Canadian Manda Group, 165 Dufferin Street
Toronto, Ontario, Canada M6K 3H6
Distributed in Australia by Capricorn Link (Australia) Pty. Ltd.
P.O. Box 704, Windsor, NSW 2756, Australia

Sterling ISBN 978-1-4027-7849-0

For information about custom editions, special sales, premium and corporate purchases, please contact Sterling Special Sales Department at 800-805-5489 or specialsales@sterlingpublishing.com.

Contents

▼ ▼ ▼ ▼ ▼ ▼ ▼ ▼ ▼

1. **F**ishy Fun

Which fish won first place on a TV reality show?

The Sole Survivor.

Knock-knock!
Who's there?
I, Nemo.
I, Nemo who?
I Nemo money so lend me some.

What did Mr. Sponge say to the big bully?
Leave me alone or I'll wipe up the ocean floor with you.

Shark computers take mega bytes.

What did the sea captain say to the pop star?
Please don't rock the boat.

And then there was the crooked merman who got arrested for starting a crime wave.

What is Corporal Octopus an expert at?
Hand to hand to hand to hand to hand to hand to hand to hand combat.

What military vehicle is found at the bottom of the ocean?
The fish tank.

Where does a clam go to lift weights?
Mussel Beach.

BOY: That building isn't a skyscraper. It's only a bait shack.
GIRL: But it has at least a hundred fish stories in it.

What do you get if you cross the ocean with a rabbit?
A wavy hare.

SEA OTTER: We need immediate assistance. We're starving.

SEAL: Relax. Kelp is on the way.

Why couldn't the little fish get a good job?
He dropped out of school before graduation.

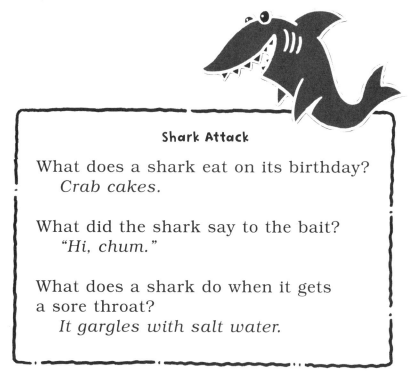

Shark Attack

What does a shark eat on its birthday?
Crab cakes.

What did the shark say to the bait?
"Hi, chum."

What does a shark do when it gets a sore throat?
It gargles with salt water.

MR. SHARK: I just came back from vacation.

MR. MARLIN: Where did you go?

MR. SHARK: Fin Land.

LOAN SHARK: Are you going to pay me in cash?

SHARKY: No. Here's a credit cod.

Mr. Sponge Riddlers

Why did Mr. Sponge go to the bank?
He wanted to float a loan.

What do you get if you cross a cabbage with Mr. Sponge?
A vegetable that soaks its head.

How did Mr. Sponge get past the crowd of tightly packed sardines?
He squeezed through.

Where does Mr. Sponge buy his groceries?
At a fish market.

Why was Junior Sponge's mom mad at him?
He came home from school soaking wet and dripped water on the floor.

TEACHER: Did you learn anything from my lecture today?
JUNIOR SPONGE: No. You talked so fast, I couldn't absorb anything.

Why did Mr. Sponge go to Hollywood?
To visit his friend who is a starfish.

What does Mr. Sponge
use to call home?
  A shell phone.

How does Mr. Sponge
cook a meal quickly?
  *He uses a
  microwave oven.*

What did Mr. Sponge say to
his girlfriend?
  "You're my main squeeze."

What does Mr. Sponge do when he has
a cold?
  He takes in plenty of fluids.

Does Mr. Sponge take a bus to work?
  No. He goes by taxi crab.

How does Mr. Sponge relax after
a hard day?
  He soaks in a hot tub.

What does Mr. Sponge wear on his
head?
  A fishing derby.

Is Mr. Sponge too chubby?
  No. He just has a lot of water weight.

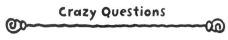

Does a flounder like sole food?

Do teenage mermaids like to throw swim parties?

What kind of fish can't keep a secret?
One that has a tattle tail.

What kind of candy does the ocean eat?
Saltwater taffy.

Who makes the best seafood—fish or clams?
Fish can fry, but clams can bake.

What did King Neptune do in the stands at the baseball game?
He started a wave.

Who keeps King Neptune's castle clean?
The mermaids.

Daffynitions

BEACH EROSION—a case of bad tidings
BAITING THE HOOK—a catchphrase

What kind of whales do you find off the coast of Scotland?
Kilter whales.

Why do little fish like storms?
Because schools are closed during bad weather.

Why do fish make bad baseball pitchers?
Because they hate to be caught.

MERMAN: I visited a nightclub at the bottom of the ocean.
MERMAID: Was it a nice place?
MERMAN: No, It was a reel dive.

FISH #1: Why are you so dizzy?
FISH #2: Because I just took a tailspin.

Who is the dumbest whale in the ocean?
Moby-Dork.

What did the boy octopus say to the girl squid?

"Can I put my arms around you?"

Who guides a ship, is green, and has sharp teeth?

The navi-gator.

Where does a sardine go when it feels sick?

To the school nurse.

What did Mr. Fish wear to the office?

A bathing suit and tie.

MERMAID: Am I pretty or not?
MERMAN: Quit fishing for a compliment.

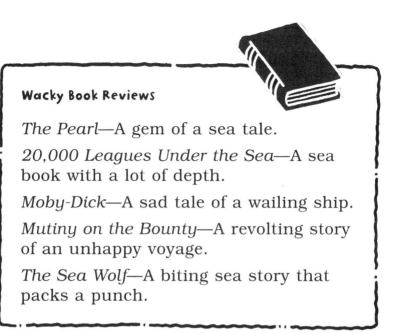

Wacky Book Reviews

The Pearl—A gem of a sea tale.

20,000 Leagues Under the Sea—A sea book with a lot of depth.

Moby-Dick—A sad tale of a wailing ship.

Mutiny on the Bounty—A revolting story of an unhappy voyage.

The Sea Wolf—A biting sea story that packs a punch.

MR. BASS: I didn't see Mr. Tuna at work today.
MR. COD: He got canned yesterday.

Where does a fish farmer keep his tiny sea cow? *In a barnacle.*

MERMAN #1: Did you ever ride on a dolphin by mistake?
MERMAN #2: No. But once I took a ride on porpoise.

MR. CRAB: What are your future plans?
MR. LOBSTER: To stay out of hot water if I can.

MINNOW: Why is the nurse shark visiting our school?
SARDINE: She's going to give us a herring test.

What did the bass yell to his friend at the intersection?
  "Turn, pike!"

MARLIN: Why are you so grouchy? Is it something you ate?
SHARK: I'm not sure. I guess it could be the crab in me.

MINNOW: What is your favorite sport?
GUPPY: Bowl-ing.

Attention!

Flying fish are found in high schools.

Smart fish know a lot about current events.

What's the easiest job in the ocean?
  Being a lifeguard. Everyone there knows how to swim.

FISH #1: I'm riding the waves from England to France.
FISH #2: Oh, why don't you quit channel surfing.

Daffynitions

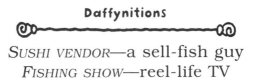

SUSHI VENDOR—a sell-fish guy
FISHING SHOW—reel-life TV

MAN: Hey! There's no bait on your line. What kind of fish do you expect to catch?
BOY: One that isn't hungry.

What do you get if you cross a fishing rod with Batman?
A reel superhero.

FISHERMAN: I caught this sea bass by accident.
CAPTAIN: For your information, it's just a fluke.

CHARTER BOAT CAPTAIN: Would you like to come fishing with us free of charge?
MAN: What's the catch?

Sign on a Shipbuilder's Factory
Check out our sail items!

Knock-knock!
Who's there?
Eel.
Eel who?
Eel miss the boat if he doesn't hurry.

Show me a mate who swims through an oil spill...and I'll show you a sea-slick sailor!

MARTY: I went ice fishing.
ARTY: What did you catch?
MARTY: Frozen fish.

Want Ad
Dockworkers needed—
we provide free pier counseling.

Stars of Fishing Shows

Rod N. Reel
Moe Torboat
Ivan Fishin
Annette S. Handy

MATT: I wrote a play about fishermen.
PAT: Can I be in the cast?
MATT: How are you when it comes to your
    lines?
PAT: Reel good.

Knock-knock!
  Who's there?
I, Lloyd.
  I, Lloyd who?
I Lloyd when I said I caught a big fish.

What did the little sea scallop say?
  "I may be small, but I'm not
  a shrimp."

2.
Pirate Treasures

▼ ▼

MATE: Captain Morgan, I want my back pay right now.

CAPTAIN MORGAN: Okay, but I'm short of cash. I'll have to give you a check, mate.

CAPTAIN MORGAN: Hey, matey! What's the name of that thing floating in the ocean off the coast of Ireland?

MATE: Danny Buoy.

Why do basketball players make bad pirates?
They always jump ship.

Why did the pirate go to the eye doctor?
Arr, he kept seeing bleary treasure.

What did the pirate say to his hives?
"Avast bee hearties!"

Which nasty bug is a famous pirate?
Long John Silverfish.

What is a pirate's favorite fast food?
Pizzas of eight.

Who sails with Captain Niblet?
His buccaneers of corn.

How do pirates wash their clothes during a long voyage?
They sail with the Tide laundry soap.

How can you tell which treasure belongs to Super Pirate?
There'll be an S on his chest.

Which pirate got into trouble for not going to school?
Captain Hooky.

CAPTAIN: What do you see through that telescope?
MATE: A big ship with a lot of rabbits on deck.
CAPTAIN: It must be a hare-craft carrier.

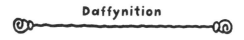

Daffynition

WALK THE PLANK—a pirate's board game

Which tree is a famous buccaneer?
Barkbeard the Pirate.

What does Santa Pirate yell?
"Yo-ho-ho-ho!"

What does a pirate say when he works in his garden?
"Yo-hoe-hoe-hoe!"

What kind of strange noises did the pirate hear?

Ear rings.

How did the pirate leader get a washboard stomach?

He did a lot of captain crunches.

Did you hear about the pirate captain who sailed his ship to the Arctic Ocean just so he could shiver his timbers?

Why did the lovesick pirate go to sea?

To search for his perfect mate.

Which pirate do fish fear the most?

Captain Hook.

Which sheep is a famous sea captain?

Sinbaa Baa the Sailor.

What grades did the little pirate get on his report card?

Seven C's.

3

Computer Chuckles

▼ ▼

How do you use a computer on the bottom floor of an elevator?

Dial it up, up, up.

What do you get if you cross a computer shopping service with cute lifeguards?

eBay-Watch.

What sound does a computerized clock make?

Tech! Tech! Tech!

How do you send an electronic message to a hive?

Use bee mail.

ANN: I have a goose feather computer.
DAN: What kind of computer is that?
ANN: One that makes it easy to download stuff.

Where does a computer go when it gets a virus?

To the doc of eBay.

What did the computer have for breakfast?
Spam and eggs.

What did the computer whiz say to eBay?
"I don't need help, I'm just browsing."

Knock-knock!
Who's there?
Icon.
Icon who?
Icon hear you, so stop knocking.

What did the stressed-out computer say?
"I can't take disk anymore."

Attention!

Snobby computer users have their own
special cliques.

007: I know a spy who had an electronic
device so tiny, he could hide it in his
mustache.
008: What kind of device was it?
007: A liptop computer.

Where's the best place to find a donkey on
the Internet?
Try eBray.

How do you catch a computer fish?
Use the Internet.

Chat Roomers

Knock-knock!
  Who's there?
M. T.
  M. T. who?
M. T. headed hackers.

        Knock-knock!
          Who's there?
        I-M-A-B.
          I-M-A-B who?
        I-M-A-B keeper. Buzz. Buzz.

Knock-knock!
  Who's there?
C-N.
  C-N who?
C-N is believing.

        Knock-knock!
          Who's there?
        A-2-4-1.
          A-2-4-1 who?
        A-2-4-1 sale means big savings.

Knock-knock!
Who's there?
N-E.
N-E who?
N-E time S fine
with me.

Knock-knock!
Who's there?
I-8-D.
I-8-D who?
I-8-D whole cake.

Knock-knock!
Who's there?
U-R-N.
U-R-N who?
U-R-N big trouble,
dude!

Knock-knock!
Who's there?
Z-S-4.
Z-S-4 who?
Z-S-4 Zorro!

Knock-knock!
Who's there?
COM-E-D.
COM-E-D who?
COM-E-D is funny
stuff.

Knock-knock!
Who's there?
U-B.
U-B who?
U-B good now.

Knock-knock!
Who's there?
R-U.
R-U who?
R-U online?

What's the best way for a group of people to find something on the Internet?
Organize a search party.

How do you activate a chicken computer?
Cluck it on.

What did the computer masseuse send to her aching client?
An instant massage.

Daffynition

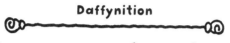

INFORMATION FEE—know charge

How do you buy a pet spider on the Internet?
Check out the Web pages.

What is a computer's favorite type of music?
Disk-go.

What is a computer lover's wedding vow?
I promise to love, honor, and eBay.

What do you get if you cross a boxer with a computer whiz?
A guy who punches his keyboard hard and fast.

What do you do if a computer uses a bad word?
Wash out its speaker with Dial soap.

JILL: I'm tired of switching from site to site on my computer.
BILL: Oh, surf bored, huh?

What do you call a chicken who likes to use a computer?
A technical fowl.

Knock-knock!
  Who's there?
Modem.
  Modem who?
Modem. Larry and Curly smart.

Attention!

Computerized robot dogs do not send flea mail!

Daffynition

APPLE COMPUTER—the fruit of rapid growth in a high-tech industry

What does a hungry modem snack on?
Computer chips.

What does a hungry modem on a diet snack on?
Microchips.

4.

It's a Nutty World

What did Oliver Twist say after he had lunch in Hawaii?

"Please, sir, now I want Samoa."

What's cute, green, and sings?

Britney Asparagus Spears.

What did the bald customer say to the toupee maker when he called him on his cell phone?

"Can you hair me now?"

ALI: Aladdin was fortunate to find a magic lamp.

BABA: Yes—he has the luck of the I wish folks.

Then there was the beaver who found a magic lamp and made tree wishes.

ALADDIN: What do you mean I have to pay airfare?

GENIE: Think of it as flying carpet tax.

Why did the jogger get a ticket?
He ran a stop sign.

What's Your Favorite Day?

"My burpday," said the soda pop.

"Thirstday," said the camel.

"The Fork of July," said the spoon.

"Stinksgiving," said the perfume.

"Valentime's Day," said the clock.

"Earth Day," said the dirt farmer.

"New Ear's Day," said the cornstalk.

"Presidentures' Day," said the dentist.

TRACY: My husband and I met while we were chasing a tornado.
STACY: Wow! Talk about a whirlwind romance.

AL: Do barbers read newspapers?
SAL: Yes. But only the headlines.

How do you babysit a calendar?
Send it to a day-care center.

MAN: Why did you name your son Calculator?
FATHER: I wanted to be sure I could count on him in the future.

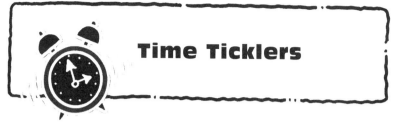

Time Ticklers

TED: My hound dog has fleas.
ED: Well, my watchdog has ticks.

JOE: What do you think of my new
　　stopwatch?
MOE: Give me a second to think.

Sign on a Watch Shop
Around-the-Clock Repairs

Then there was the dumb boxer who
punched the time clock and broke it.

CUSTOMER: Can I pick out any clock I want?
SALESMAN: Yes. Please take your own time.

My grandfather clock is so old, his time
is running out.

ZACK: I think I should have bought that
　　other watch instead of this one. I bet it
　　keeps better time.
MACK: Oh, stop second-guessing yourself.

What Did the Policeman Say to the Gangster Clocks?

"Hands up!"

"Turn around slow and face me."

"I expect a confession any minute now."

"You got caught because you set off the alarm."

"No. I won't give you a second chance."

"If you know what's good for you, you'll tock fast."

"Now you'll wind up in jail."

"If you're lucky, you'll get time off for good behavior."

MAN: Do you have time for me today?
REPAIRMAN: No, sir. Your watch won't be fixed until tomorrow.

Show me an outdated skyscraper...and I'll show you a building with lots of old stories.

JERRY: I'm going to be a famous stand-up comedian someday.
BARRY: Ha! Don't make me laugh.
LARRY: Yeah. Who are you trying to kid?

FIREMAN: The old glue factory just collapsed.
REPORTER: Is it a major disaster?
FIREMAN: No. But it's a very sticky situation.

LADY: What do you prescribe for my stuffy nose?

DOCTOR: Perfume.

LADY: What? Why perfume?

DOCTOR: It'll make you smell better.

Speak Up

MR. BATTERY: I'll take charge!

MR. LIGHT: Say watt?

MR. SCRAMBLED EGGS: Beat it, dude!

MR. CREDIT CARD: Let's talk shop.

LOIS: I just saw Superman fly by.

JIMMY: Humph! Now there's a guy with no visible means of support.

Nutty Notice

An archaeologist is a person who loves to live in the past.

What did one empty pyramid say to the other?

"I miss my mummy."

STRANGER: I'm looking for a town called Recovery.

FARMER: Turn left up yonder and you'll be on the road to Recovery.

ZACK: What's wrong?

MACK: I just had a fender bender with a police car.

ZACK: Wow! Talk about having a run-in with the law.

Daffynitions

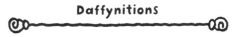

OSTRICH—a chicken who has spent years in a bodybuilding program

NUTRITIONIST—someone who knows what's good for you

BUZZ SAW—a honey of a tool

THEORY—a wise guy's hunch

SLOWPOKE—the punch of a tired boxer

CALENDAR MAKERS—a dating service

Silly Slogan

Cookbook publishers—We'll show you some dish respect.

CHILD: Someone stole my snowman.

COP: This is a job for the cold-case investigators.

BOY: Do you always collect palm leaves?

GIRL: Yes. But I can take them or weave them.

Wedded Blish

Miss Morning Mist, do you take Mr. Lawn to be your wedded husband?
I dew!

Who cleans up after the wedding ceremony?
The maid of honor.

Who married Mr. and Mrs. Green Giant?
The justice of the peas.

Mr. and Mrs. Bee went on a long honeymoon.

FATHER: My daughter, Melanie, cooks the dinner. My son, Matthew, pours the drinks. That's my son, Martin. He puts out the knives, forks, and plates.
GUEST: Oh, Martin is the setting son.
FATHER: Yes. He's my brightest child.

GIRL: Hooray! Hooray! Stir-fry those Asian vegetables, Chef!
BOY: What was that?
GIRL: A woking cheer.

Table Talk

"Pass the bread," said the quarterback.

"Is this my plate?" said the umpire.

"Fork over the lettuce," said the robber.

"My glass is half full," said the optimist.

"My glass is half empty," said the pessimist.

"My steak is medium rare," said the psychic.

Middle-earth Mirth

What vessel did the telephone pirates sail on?
The Fellowship of the Rings.

BILBO: Are you an expert at fixing
   doorbells?
ELROD: Yes. I'm the Lord of the Rings.

What do you get if you cross a rabbit with a
small person from Middle-earth?
A hoppit.

Which rock-and-roll legend was in *The Lord
of the Rings*?
Elvish Presley.

5.
X-tremely Funny

▼ ▼

What's the difference between the Easter Bunny and a great skateboard jump?
One's a big hare and the other gets big air.

When does a witch ride on a motorcycle instead of a broom?
When she's competing in the Hex Games.

Show me a stunt rider who removes his wristwatch...and I'll show you an athlete whose timing is off.

What do you get if you cross a pop singer with a skater?

A rock-and-Rollerblader.

What do you call a pig on in-line wheels?

A skate pork.

Knock-knock!

Who's there?

Yemen.

Yemen who?

Yemen! That was a cool stunt, dude!

When are waves too small for surfing?

When they're microwaves.

What do you get when a Rollerblade doesn't shave?

A skatebeard.

When is the worst time to take a cross-country motorcycle trip?

During the fall season.

LADY: I rent a room in my house to a young man who roller-skates.

MAN: It sounds to me like you have a skateboarder.

MACK: Does Luke Skywalker use a lightsaber at the X Games?

ZACK: No. He uses a Rollerblade.

FRED: When did your pet dog learn how to skateboard?

ED: Right after the neighbor's cat learned how to roller-skate.

KEN: I met my new girlfriend at a skating park.

LEN: How did you two get together?

KEN: I saw her while I was riding my board and just fell for her.

BILL: What's the difference between a surfboard ride and a skateboard ride?

PHIL: Dude, fall off one and you hear a big splash. Fall off the other and you hear a big crash!

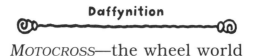

MOTOCROSS—the wheel world

Don: My stunt bike is made out of wood
instead of metal.
RON: What kind of bike is that?
DON: It a tree-wheeler.

What did the clumsy skateboarder yell
when he jumped in the air to perform a
trick?
Ollie-ooops!

SPIKE: That motorcycle driver must be new
to the sport.
MIKE: What makes you say that?
SPIKE: His bike has training wheels.

How do you get into a skate park for free?
Use a boarding pass.

Why is Tony Hawk like an Olympic diver?
They both like to jump on a board.

Knock-knock!
Who's there?
Dairy.
Dairy who?
Dairy goes, over the first jump.

6.

Animal Antics

▼ ▼

CROW: Hey, raccoon! Why are you only eating ears of corn at the bottom of the stalks?

RACCOON: I'm on a low-cob diet.

DON: Why isn't your watchdog at obedience school?

JOHN: I'm expecting unwelcome company to arrive, so he's taking a sic day.

What should you do if a goose has accident?
Call in a parameduck.

JILL: Wow! How did you make your canary sing?
BILL: I gave it a piece of candy.
JILL: What kind of candy?
BILL: A special tweet mint.

Why was the bluebird mad?
He got a ticket for jaywalking.

Knock-knock!
Who's there?
Ewe.
Ewe who?
Now, that's how a sheep yodels.

Who directs how and where rabbits drive their cars?
The hare traffic controller.

What does an alligator hear when he picks up the telephone?
The crocodile tone.

CONNIE: How's the dog grooming business?
DONNIE: It bites.

How does a veterinarian learn how to cure ill cows?
He takes moo-sick lessons.

Some policemen in the K-9 corps have patrol curs.

℗

What does a New York Yankee zebra wear?
Pin-stripes.

TIM: Want to hear a shocking story about a duck?
JIM: Sure.
TIM: Okay. Once upon a time there was a duck who had an electric bill.

What did the impatient racehorse say to the farmer?
Quit trying to stall me.

POLICEMAN: You can't raise pigs in this neighborhood.
FARMER: Why not?
POLICEMAN: It's a no-porking zone.

Silly Slogan
Bird experts—We're at your beak and call.

What do you get if you cross an ATM with a dairy farm?
Lots of cash cows.

Daffynition
℗━━━━━━━━━━━━━━━℗

GREYHOUND TRAINER—a race cur driver

Knock-knock!
   Who's there?
Gillette.
   Gillette who?
Gillette the dog out?

MR. CROW: Bring me my new suit.
LITTLE CROW: What was that?
MRS. CROW: A clothes caw.

What's woolly, travels under the ocean, and goes baa baa?
   A ewe boat.

Do rabbits lift weights?
   No. They do harerobics.

What do the Green Giant's hens lay?
Eggplants.

Then there was the tough kangaroo who got a job as a nightclub bouncer.

ATTACK DOG TO TRAINER: I hate you. You make me sic.

ANN: I named my dog Magician.
JAN: Why? Does he do magic tricks?
ANN: Just watch. Magician, vanish!
JAN: Doggone!

Notice

Invest in a pig farm and put your fortune in good hams.

Which farm animal always cheats at hide-and-seek?
The peeking duck.

Barnyard Reports

"I'm not interested in a gallop poll," said the horse.

"If you edit out my comments, I'll consider it a slop in the face," said the pig.

"Whenever I do an interview, I end up with egg on my face," said the hen.

"This is udder nonsense," said the cow.

What do you get if you cross a variety of fish with an egg-laying mammal?
A seafood platypus.

Crazy Question
Do business crows carry cawing cards?

Which tree supports animal rights?
The fake fir tree.

What do you get if you cross a turtle with a goose and the speed limit?
A slow-down zone.

Why did the Lion King lose his golf match?
His opponent was Tiger Woods.

7.
Ghostly Giggles

Why did the ghost haunt Albert Einstein for ten years?

It took that long to scare all the wits out of him.

GHOST: How did you like me in my last horror movie?

CRITIC: You were terrible! Horrible! Awful!

GHOST: Ah, it's nice to be appreciated.

How do computer ghosts contact each other?
Eeek mail.

What is Little Dracula's favorite book?
The Bat in the Hat.

What is a ghost's favorite TV reality show?
Fear Factor.

What's the main ingredient of spooky pizza?
Weird dough.

GHOSTWRITER: I penned a story about a vampire snowman.
GHOST: What's it called?
GHOSTWRITER: *Biting Cold.*

Why did the mad scientist name his monster Zero?
Because he was afraid of nothing.

What kind of weather do ghosts like?
Boo skies.

GHOST SAILOR: Is this haunted ship really manned by ghosts?
GHOST CAPTAIN: Yes. What did you expect, a skeleton crew?

What did the English ghost say after he accidentally scared King Richard?
"Frightfully sorry, sire."

Ghostwriter News

"My story is a haunting saga."

"RIP—Read It, Please."

"My doctor is mad about this book."

"You can really sink your teeth into the chapter about vampires."

"It has a killer cast of characters."

"I'm dying to write a sequel."

"My writing career was at a dead end until this book gave it new life."

"I hope it doesn't get buried in the bookstore."

What Did the Critics Say?

"I'm afraid I don't like the burial plot."

"It has no shelf life at all."

"It has some grave editing problems."

"RIP—this book is so awful, it should be shredded and rest in pieces."

Daffynition

EXORCISM—the unspoken word

How do you build a haunted house?
Follow the boo prints.

What did the sailor shout when he spotted the ghost whale?
"Thar she boos."

What kind of ghosts live in magic lamps?
Boo genies.

Where does an unexpected guest ghost sleep?
On a fraidy cot.

Attention!

General Ghost tried to win the war by using scare tactics.

A ghost went to see a fortune-teller. "How are you?" asked the ghost.

"I'm in good spirits today," replied the medium.

What does a ghost use on his computer monitor?

A scream saver.

How do you spook a horse?

Show it a ghost.

What's soft and yellow and scary?

Winnie the Boo.

LADY: I saw a small ghost.
MAN: Was it a big shock?
LADY: No. But I was a little afraid.

Want Ad

Ghost actors needed—must be able to perform before a live audience.

What do you get when a ghost vows not to speak?

Dead silence.

What fantasy creature is messy and scary?
The Slob Goblin.

Why is a haunted house always dark?
Ghosts scare the daylights out of it.

What does Jesse James Ghost wear on his head?
A cowbooey hat.

TIM: Are you really a ghost?
SPIRIT: I'm afraid so.
TIM: No. I'm the one who's afraid.

Knock-knock!
  Who's there?
Cat's purr.
  Cat's purr who?
Cat's purr the friendly ghost.

GHOST CAPTAIN: Are your men discouraged?
GHOST SERGEANT: No, sir! There's still some
   fright left in them.

What did the ghost sports fan sing on his
way to South Bend, Indiana?
  "Fright, Fright for Ol' Notre Dame."

Attention!

Ghost soldiers don't crawl, they creep
   forward.

Before they can fly well, new vampires have
   to take batting practice.

The Wolfman likes to wear a houndstooth
   jacket.

Ghost fighter pilots fly Phantom jets.

8.
Knocking Around

▼ ▼

Knock-knock!
Who's there?
Brandy.
Brandy who?
Brandy steers with
a branding iron,
cowboy.

Knock-knock!
Who's there?
Kobe.
Kobe who?
Kobe or not kobe,
that is the
question.

Knock-knock!
  Who's there?
Shaq.
  Shaq who?
Shaq, rattle, and roll.

Knock-knock!
  Who's there?
Ewe.
  Ewe who?
Ewe go, girl!

Knock-knock!
  Who's there?
Wanda.
  Wanda who?
Wanda around, you'll find a place to camp.

Knock-knock!
  Who's there?
Oil.
  Oil who?
Oil have the blue plate special.

Knock-knock!
  Who's there?
Soda.
  Soda who?
Soda Mets are finally in the World Series.

Knock-knock!
  Who's there?
Dish.
  Dish who?
Dish is the end of dish story.

Knock-knock!
  Who's there?
Bean, dear.
  Bean, dear who?
Bean dear, done that.

Knock-knock!
Who's there?
Milt Ed.
Milt Ed who?
Milt Ed cheese
tastes good.

Knock-knock!
Who's there?
Egos.
Egos who?
Egos are big birds
of prey.

Knock-knock!
Who's there?
Yoda.
Yoda who?
Yoda one who
makes my dream
come true.

Knock-knock!
Who's there?
Wits.
Wits who?
Wits the problem,
won't your key
work?

Knock-knock!
  Who's there?
Heaven.
  Heaven who?
Heaven you fixed
this door yet?

Knock-knock!
  Who's there?
Gwenyth.
  Gwenyth who?
Gwenyth the train
due to arrive?

Knock-knock!
  Who's there?
Hugh Carey.
  *Hugh Carey
  who?*
Hugh Carey that
suitcase and I'll
get this one.

Knock-knock!
  Who's there?
Toupee.
  Toupee who?
Toupee the
admission price
and the third one
gets in free.

Knock-knock!
  Who's there?
Alma.
  Alma who?
Alma money is
tied up in
municipal bonds.

Knock-knock!
  Who's there?
Ooma.
  Ooma who?
Ooma hand hurts
  from all this
    knocking.

9.
Funny Business

▼ ▼

MR. GREEN: My company produces live bait for fishermen all over the world.

MR. BROWN: What's it called?

MR. GREEN: Global worming.

Show me a group of people discussing insect hives...and I'll show you a bees' nest meeting.

Which secret agent works as a department store Santa?

James Bond—Double Ho Ho Seven.

Which supercool spy cleans up after a snowstorm?
Austin Plowers.

Knock-knock!
Who's there?
Jewel.
Jewel who?
Jewel be sorry if you quit this job.

BUSINESSMAN: Let's form a committee to build a new dock.
BUSINESSWOMAN: Okay. I always wanted to be in a pier group.

Why Are You Late?

"I got held up," said the banker.

"I was tied up," said the rope salesman.

"I was under the weather," said the meteorologist.

"I had car trouble," said the mechanic.

"I didn't get up on time," said the clock maker.

Daffynition

CORRAL ENTERPRISES—a company with a lot of stockholders

The Gas House Gang

Phil Earup

Flip D. Hood

Anita Tuneup

Emanuel Transmission

MR. SMITH: What do you do for a living?
MR. JONES: I'm a salesman.
MR. SMITH: What does your wife do for a living?
MR. JONES: She's a saleswoman.
MR. SMITH: I guess that makes you two sell mates.

FOREMAN: Please remove all wristwatches before entering the factory.

NEW WORKER: Wow! I like this job. I just got here and they're already telling me to take time off.

Notice

People who sell flood insurance need a dry sense of humor.

Then there was the chicken who got a job at a big hotel and worked as a desk cluck.

Then there was the CEO who loved surfing, so he took his board to the beach.

Job Hunters

Beautiful models needed...we pay face value.

Mad doctor needed...to teach anger management course.

BOSS: If I put you in charge of the store, there's a lot to do. Can you handle it?

WORKER: Don't worry, I'll manage.

TINA: My money is in porkers.

GINA: Hog farms?

TINA: No. Piggy banks.

Show me a man thinking about investing in real estate...and I'll show you a man with lots on his mind.

ZACK: I'm investing in a cattle ranch.
MACK: Now, that's a bull market.

COMPANY PRESIDENT: It was a difficult decision to make. Thirty people applied for the job of vice president, and I could only pick one. I selected the best person for the job based on his outstanding qualifications. It's Mr. Jason Morgan. What do you say to that, Mr. Morgan?
MR. MORGAN: Ya-hoo! Thanks, Dad!

What do you get if you cross a guy who carries golf clubs with a seven-foot basketball star?

Caddy Shaq.

MAN #1: I work as a groundskeeper at a golf course.

MAN #2: Is it a difficult job?

MAN #1: It has its rough moments.

Daffynitions

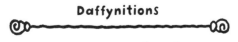

PENNY BANK—a wee fund account

CRATE MANUFACTURERS—case workers

Want Ads

Hotel custodian needed—lots of rooms for
  improvement.

Person needed to fill salt and pepper
  shakers at restaurant—seasonal work.

Apprentice truck driver needed—before long,
  you'll be going places on the road to
  success.

HOME BUYER: I've looked at so many houses
  for sale, I'm starting to see double.
REALTOR: Nah! That's just a duplex.

What is the favorite game of sale items?
  Price tag.

Crazy Question
Do lumberjacks have to log on at work?

WORKER: What do you think of our new
  advertising campaign to sell jogging shoes?
CLIENT: I'm not sure. Run it by me again.

Knock-knock!
  Who's there?
Wade.
  Wade who?
Wade until tomorrow to ask for a raise.

Sign on the All-Sorts Bank
Our safe has a winning
combination!

Job Hunters

Become a hotel clerk—check us out.

Become a professional photographer—
picture yourself working for us!

Become a fitness instructor—this job is
guaranteed to work out.

Become a state lottery worker—this is the
chance you've been waiting for!

BUSINESSMAN: Hooray! Hooray! Let's start
this meeting.
STOCKHOLDER #1: Who is that guy?
STOCKHOLDER #2: He's the cheerman of the
board.

Notices

Invest in land sales and you'll be glad you
deed.

Invest in a trash compactor company—buy
junk bonds.

Invest in sugarcane—it's a sweet deal.

Invest in our road map company—we'll
never steer you wrong.

APPLICANT: What's it like to work here at the Ace Novelty Company?
PERSONNEL DIRECTOR: When it comes to making money, we don't joke around.

Want Ads

Bounty hunters needed—rewarding work.

Person needed to comb hair in barbershop—part time.

PETER: Do angels make good employees?
PAUL: Yes. They're miracle workers.

MAN: Where do you work?
WOMAN: At the wool sweater factory.
MAN: How is the union there?
WOMAN: It's a tightly knit group.

Job Descriptions

BABYSITTER—a person whose work schedule changes frequently.

GYM TEACHER—a person who sweats out her job every day.

MAIL CARRIER—A person who pushes the envelopes.

Loony Lawyers

Mr. Will N. Testament

Mr. Hy Court

Ms. L. Sue Anybody

Mr. Manny Trials

Mr. Al Object

Knock-knock!
Who's there?
Reveal.
Reveal who?
Reveal we deserve a raise.

Want Ads

People needed to clear snow—take this job and shovel it.

Snowplow drivers—make some cold cash.

10.
The Merry Media

▼ ▼

What kind of television programs do yaks like?

Musk-see TV.

SAL: I'm watching an old tape of the Boston Marathon.

HAL: How can you enjoy viewing a rerun?

DIRECTOR: Doughnut Commercial.

BOX OF DOUGHNUTS: Take two!

The Kooky TV Critics

"I question the value of TV quiz shows."

"There should be a law against violent police shows."

"Sci-fi shows just take up programming space."

"Reality shows are unreal."

Friends of the Meteorologist

Wayne E. Day

Cole Front

Sonny Mourning

Claire N. Coole

Tamara S. Better

Show Time

The Pie Cooking Show—a slice-of-life program

The Ghost Cop Show—*NYPD Boo*

Tornado TV—the real whirl

ACTOR: I'm the star of a new play called *Petty Theft.*
PRESS AGENT: Are you any good in it?
ACTOR: I steal every scene.

How Did You Like That New Hospital Show?

"It made me sick."

"It needs an emergency rewrite."

"I don't have the heart to tell you."

"It was painful to watch."

"The leading man is such a bad actor, they should 'doc' his pay."

"It's a bitter pill to swallow."

PRODUCER: How would you like to star in a television program about a commercial airline?

ACTOR: Oh, boy! A TV pilot at last.

ACTRESS: We named our new baby Channels.

REPORTER: Uh-oh! It sounds like the baby is crying.

ACTRESS: I guess it's time for me to change Channels.

Notice

Atlas won a Best Supporting Actor for his role in *Mythology*.

ACTOR: I play a lumberjack in this movie.

REPORTER: What do you do in it?

ACTOR: I chop down trees.

REPORTER: When do you do that?

ACTOR: When the director yells, "Cut!"

What is the top TV quiz show in the Banana Republic?

The Peel of Fortune.

Daffynitions

MAD TV—a place to channel your rage

WACKY GAME SHOWS—loco broadcasting

JONI: I was hired to work on a soap opera.
TONI: Now's your chance to clean up your act.

AGENT: What type of act do you fellas do?
BOB: I sing.
ROB: I tell really dumb jokes and play stupid.
AGENT: Oh, you're a song-and-dunce team.

Check the Channel

The Snake Show—E-Hiss-PN

The Farm Show—Hay-BC

The Ocean Show—Sea-BS

The Vegetable Show—Pea-BS

The Poultry Show—Hen-BC

11.
Fitness Fun

▼ ▼

What did the tardy jogger say as he passed an old friend?

I can't stop to talk, I'm running late today.

How do cattle stay in shape?

They exercise on a steer climber.

What did the angry baseball umpire shout to the bald coach?

You're outta hair!

Want Ad
Radio sports announcer needed—must be able to talk a good game.

What race did Seabiscuit win?
The fishing derby.

Which sports channel does a poultry farmer watch?
ESP-Hen.

Baseball star Swede Chariot went into the game to pinch-hit. The hurler for the other team was throwing knee-high fastballs. The hitter's coach yelled out this advice to his player: "Swing low, Swede Chariot!"

Notice
They crossed a marching band with the pep club and got musical cheers!

Where does a golf instructor work?
At a driving school.

Show me a businessman who produces blankets for football players who catch passes...and I'll show you a guy who covers wide receivers.

Show me a hockey player with her skates on...and I'll show you a slipshod athlete.

DIET PLANNER—a fast talker
INFIELD DIRT—double play ground
ENGLISH WRESTLING CHAMPION—a lord of the ring
GOOD GOLF WEATHER—a decent forecast

What's the best way to ship a baseball hitter?

Put him in a batter's box and take him to the post office.

Show me a frog who plays basketball...and I'll show you a player with a good jump shot.

Notice

When telemarketers play touch football,
everyone wants to be the signal caller.

ED: Hey, Joe! What's that foaming out of
that soda bottle?
JOE: Relax! It's fizz, Ed.

MEL: Why are you so upset?
DELL: I want to run track, but when it comes
to jumping the first hurdle I'm afraid.
MEL: Relax, you'll get over it.

BOSS: Does Jack the custodian play on the
company softball team?
COACH: Yes. He's our cleanup batter.

Daffynition

WOMEN'S PROFESSIONAL BOXING—
a punch-at-Judy show

Want Ad

Gymnastics teacher needed—flexible work
schedule.

WITCH: I put a hex on a golfer and he made
a hole in one.
WIZARD: Is that par for the curse?

12.
Making the Goofy Grade at School

▼ ▼

BILLY: I was a top student in bunk-bed school. How about you?
WILLIE: I was an undergraduate.

TILLIE: How did you learn to slow-cook a bunch of small fish?
MILLIE: I took a simmer-school class.

THE X-FILES—the mystery of algebra

Show me a geometry whiz...and I'll show
you a student who thinks she
knows all the angles.

TEACHER: Today we're going to watch a film
about exploring the ocean bottom.
STUDENT: Oh, boy! A dive-in movie.

Silly Slogans

Lumberjack school—If you come here, try
cutting class!

Ace Cooking School—Our graduates have to
pass a taste test.

TEACHER: Do you like sewing class?
STUDENT: Yes. It's tailor-made for me.

SISTER: Did you do your addition homework
on Thursday?
LITTLE BROTHER: No.
SISTER: Did you do your addition homework
on Friday?
LITTLE BROTHER: No.
SISTER: Did you do your addition homework
on Saturday?
LITTLE BROTHER: No. Why?
SISTER: Because Sum-day you'll be sorry.

Lumberjack school tutor—If chopping
   homework has you stumped, ax for me.

BOY: My teacher doesn't know the difference
   between math and grammar.
MOM: What makes you think that?
BOY: She keeps talking about add-verbs.

TEACHER: Did you think band class would be
   all fun?
STUDENT: Yes. I only came here to play.

Notice
A student needs good motor skills to pass
   auto shop.

Hey, Substitute Teacher!

"Can you teach ancient history?"
"Sure. I've had past experience."

"Can you teach gym class?"
"No sweat!"

"How are you at teaching geology?"
"Rock solid."

"Can you teach algebra?"
"No problem."

"Can you teach Spanish?"
"Just sí if I can."

"Can you teach English grammar?"
"Sure. It ain't hard."

What do you get if you cross an art teacher with a math instructor?
A color-by-numbers project.

MAN #1: What's your line of work?
MAN #2: I'm a fence maker with a postgraduate degree.

BOY: How was my paper on the ocean? Was it good enough to get an A?
TEACHER: No. It was only C-worthy.

13.
Countryside Splitters

Show me a farmer with a bag of seeds in the middle of a city...and I'll show you a man with no place to grow.

POLITICIAN: How can we tell if farmers want to grow hay this summer?
ASSISTANT: Take a straw poll.

What rock-and-roll star plays guitar at the hive?
Johnny Bee Good.

What did one cool bee say to the other?
Hi, pal! Give me a hive five.

Why did the farmer hire a schoolteacher?
He needed someone to grade his fruit.

FIREFLY: Ouch!
MOTH: What's wrong?
FIREFLY: Glowing pains.

FARMER: Son, tomorrow I want you to fertilize all the cornfields.
SON: Ah, Dad, that job stinks!

Knock-knock!
Who's there?
Gwen.
Gwen who?
Gwen do you milk the cows?

Silly Slogan
Sheep farm—We believe in profit shearing.

 **Notice**
Young farmers are green recruits.

MAN #1: How did you get to the state fair?
MAN #2: I rode a hog.
MAN #1: You mean you rode a Harley-Davidson motorcycle?
MAN #2: No. I rode a hog. I'm a pig farmer.

Knock-knock!
  Who's there?
Garden.
  Garden who?
Garden sheep from wolves is dangerous.

For Sale

Farmland—dirt cheap

Show me a shepherd who doesn't do a good job when the sun goes down...and I'll show you a man with a lot of sheepless nights.

SCIENTIST: We artificially produce this honey without the help of insects. How would you rate it?
FARMER: Bee-minus.

COUNTRY SINGER: My next song is called "How to Make Corn Grow Fast."
FARMER: That'll be music to our ears.

FARMER: How are we going to get all this hay in the loft before it rains?
FIELD HAND: Don't worry, we'll all pitch in.

FARMER: Are you here to paint bales of hay?
ARTIST: No, I'm here to draw straws.

What kind of car does a mad bull drive?
  A snort utility vehicle.

Knock-knock!
> *Who's there?*

I, Fred.
> *I, Fred who?*

I Fred the chickens.

What did the farmer say to his farmhand, Johnny B. Good?
> *Grow, Johnny, Grow! Grow!*

FARMER: I went to college to learn how to grow straw.
RANGER: Which college?
FARMER: Hay U.

Daffynition

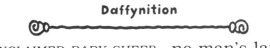

UNCLAIMED BABY SHEEP—no man's lamb

CITY FELLA: I thought farmers wake up early.

FARMER: Well, I always wake up before dawn.

CITY FELLA: Are you serious? It's noon and you just woke up.

FARMER: True. But Dawn is my wife, and she's still sleeping.

FARMER #1: That rooster always crows when he senses trouble.

FARMER #2: Maybe he's an alarm cluck.

SLIM: Did you hear about the two farmers on tractors who had a bad accident?

JIM: No. What happened?

SLIM: They plowed right into each other.

Attention!

Invest in farm produce and you can sit back and watch your money grow.

What do you call a hen custodian?
A chicken super.

GRAPE GROWER: Did you hear the joke about the wine bottle?
FARMER: Yes. It was a real corker.

What's the dumbest fruit in the orchard?
The pear of idiots

MAN: Phew! I spent the entire day picking small purple fruit.
FARMER: So?
MAN: Now I'm plum tuckered out.

14.
Feeling Good

▼ ▼

PATIENT: What's the most important thing I
   need to know about my amnesia?
DOCTOR: Don't forget to pay my bill.

   Knock-knock!
      Who's there?
   Destiny.
      Destiny who?
   Destiny that needs an operation, Doc. The
   other knee is fine.

Aladdin became a doctor and now, with the help of his magic lamp, he wishes people well!

NURSE: This patient is a kindergarten student with a slight temperature.
DOCTOR: Don't worry. It's just a low-grade fever.

PATIENT: I had to be out of my mind to come here.
PSYCHOLOGIST: Probably.

DOCTOR: I'd like to learn if you gained any pounds since you last visited me.
PATIENT: Okay. Where should I go?
DOCTOR: Back to the weighting room.

Notice
Army doctors promote good health!

Daffynitions

PEDIATRICIAN—a doctor who caters to a small group of people
OPTOMETRIST—a person you have to see
PHARMACIST—a piller of the community

DOCTOR: Little girl, why are you sticking your tongue out at me? Are you sick?
LITTLE GIRL: No. I just don't like you.

What did the doctor tell the sick flower?
"Stay in your bed for at least a week."

DENTIST: Did you do well in medical school?
DERMATOLOGIST: No. I graduated by the skin
   of my teeth.

Why did the magician go to a chiropractor?
He had a trick knee.

Daffynition

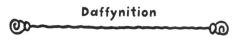

DOCTOR—a person who tries hard not to let
   her job make her sick

HOSPITAL NURSE: What's wrong, Captain? Are
   you feeling sick again?
CAPTAIN: No. I'm mad that they put me in a
   private room.

15.
Gigglers' Grab Bag

What kind of corn do they grow in Texas?
Texas Range Ears.

What do they say at the dinner table in New Hampshire?
New Hampshire tastes better than old ham.

Which colleges do smart plants attend?
Ivy League schools.

Attention, Soldiers!

"Fall in," said Major Swimming Pool.

"Hop to it," said Captain Kangaroo.

"Present arms," said Sergeant Biceps.

"Eyes right," said Lieutenant Optometrist.

"Fall out," said Colonel Balding.

"At ease," said General Comfort.

For Sale

Tunneling equipment—far below cost

Which silly state is best known for long baseball hits?
Oklahomer.

Which fish plays soccer?
The goal fish.

Show me a grumpy meteorologist who dates a grouchy weather girl...and I'll show you a stormy relationship.

Knock-knock!
Who's there?
Rio.
Rio who?
Rio funny, wise guy. You know it's me.

"I have no ill feelings," said the doctor.

"It's a grate day," said the cheese grinder.

"I could jump for joy," said the basketball player.

"Everything is in perfect harmony," said the leader of the chorus.

WIFE: Did you remember to bring home a bag of ice?
HUSBAND: No, dear. It slipped my mind.

Book Authors

How to Collect Overdue Bills—
by Cindy Money

*The Story of Archery—*by Beau N. Harrow

*The Jogger's Handbook—*by Ron A. Round

*How to Tell Dumb Jokes—*by Stu Pitt

RABBI: What is that heavenly smell?
MINISTER: It's scent from above.

Silly Song

"Jumping Jack Flashlight," by the Rolling
Blackouts

Which state is in the stage cast of a famous
Broadway play?
Montana and the King of Siam.

What did the river say to the ocean when
the salmon arrived?
"I can't talk now. My mouth is full of fish."

Which royal bird was a merry old soul?
Old King Crow.

Which state can vanish in an instant?
Oregon in a puff of smoke.

CAL: I'm on a jump-rope diet.
HAL: What kind of diet is that?
CAL: One that makes it easy to skip eating
between-meal snacks.

SCIENTIST: I failed nine times at making a
perfect cat robot, but this time I know
my little robot will be a success.
REPORTER: What do you call this robot?
SCIENTIST: Kit-ten.

Bye-Bye
"I'll catch you later," said the bounty
hunter.

"I'm outta hair," said the bald guy.

Index

▼ ▼ ▼ ▼ ▼ ▼